CHECKERBOARD BIOGRAPHY LIBRARY

U.S. PRESIDENTS

The
United States Presidents

FRANKLIN D. ROOSEVELT

ABDO Publishing Company

Megan M. Gunderson

visit us at
www.abdopublishing.com

Published by ABDO Publishing Company, 8000 West 78th Street, Edina, Minnesota 55439.
Copyright © 2009 by Abdo Consulting Group, Inc. International copyrights reserved in all
countries. No part of this book may be reproduced in any form without written permission from the
publisher. The Checkerboard Library™ is a trademark and logo of ABDO Publishing Company.

Printed in the United States.

Cover Photo: Getty Images
Interior Photos: Alamy pp. 11, 17, 29; AP Images pp. 10, 22, 25; Corbis p. 5; Getty Images pp. 9, 14;
    iStockphoto p. 32; Library of Congress pp. 24, 26; National Archives p. 27;
    Photo Researchers p. 21; Picture History pp. 13, 19

Editor: BreAnn Rumsch
Art Direction & Cover Design: Neil Klinepier
Interior Design: Neil Klinepier

Library of Congress Cataloging-in-Publication Data

Gunderson, Megan M., 1981-
  Franklin D. Roosevelt / Megan M. Gunderson.
     p. cm. -- (The United States presidents)
  Includes index.
  ISBN 978-1-60453-472-6
  1. Roosevelt, Franklin D. (Franklin Delano), 1882-1945--Juvenile literature. 2. Presidents--United
States--Biography--Juvenile literature. I. Title.
  E807.G845 2009
  973.917092--dc22
  [B]

                2008039219

CONTENTS

FRANKLIN D. ROOSEVELT

Franklin D. Roosevelt was the thirty-second president of the United States. As president, he faced difficult personal and national challenges.

Roosevelt grew up in New York. He worked as a lawyer and a state senator. Roosevelt then served as assistant secretary of the navy.

At age 39, Roosevelt became ill with **polio**. This disease **paralyzed** his legs, so he could no longer walk without help. Yet Roosevelt fought to continue in politics. He soon became governor of New York. Then in 1932, he was elected president.

As president, Roosevelt successfully led the nation through two of the worst problems of the 1900s. When he took office, the country was facing the **Great Depression**. His plans helped create jobs and improve the **economy**. President Roosevelt also led the country through **World War II**. His leadership helped end the war.

In all, Roosevelt was elected president four times. He served longer than any other president. Roosevelt became one of the most important presidents in U.S. history.

Franklin D. Roosevelt

TIMELINE

1882 - On January 30, Franklin Delano Roosevelt was born in Hyde Park, New York.

1905 - On March 17, Roosevelt married Anna Eleanor Roosevelt.

1907 - Roosevelt became a lawyer.

1910 - Roosevelt was elected to the New York state senate.

1912 - Roosevelt won reelection to the New York state senate; he worked for Woodrow Wilson's presidential election campaign.

1913 - President Wilson appointed Roosevelt assistant secretary of the navy.

1920 - Roosevelt ran for vice president under Ohio governor James M. Cox, but they lost.

1921 - Roosevelt became ill with polio.

1927 - To help other sufferers of polio, Roosevelt formed the Georgia Warm Springs Foundation.

1928 - Roosevelt was elected governor of New York.

1933 - On March 4, Roosevelt became the thirty-second U.S. president; during the Hundred Days, Roosevelt's New Deal created the Agricultural Adjustment Administration, the Civilian Conservation Corps, and the Tennessee Valley Authority.

1935 - The Second New Deal created the Works Progress Administration, the Social Security Act, and the Wagner Act.

1941 - Roosevelt's Lend-Lease Act became law on March 11; on December 7, Japan attacked the United States at Pearl Harbor in Hawaii; the following day, the United States entered World War II.

1945 - On April 12, President Franklin D. Roosevelt died.

DID YOU KNOW?

President Franklin D. Roosevelt appointed the first female cabinet member in U.S. history. Frances Perkins served as secretary of labor from 1933 to 1945.

Henry A. Wallace was Roosevelt's vice president from 1941 to 1945. During Roosevelt's first two terms, Wallace had served as secretary of agriculture. Wallace returned to Roosevelt's cabinet as secretary of commerce in 1945.

Roosevelt was a lifelong stamp collector. By the time he died, Roosevelt had more than 1 million stamps! They filled 150 albums.

Roosevelt's first inauguration took place on March 4. Then in 1933, the Twentieth Amendment to the U.S. Constitution passed. This moved inauguration day to January 20. Roosevelt took the oath of office his second, third, and fourth times on this date.

PRESIDENT OF THE
POTUS
UNITED STATES

YOUNG FRANKLIN

Franklin Delano Roosevelt was born in Hyde Park, New York, on January 30, 1882. His parents were James and Sara Delano Roosevelt.

The Roosevelts lived on a large estate along the Hudson River. James was a wealthy landowner and a railroad businessman. He was also a diplomat under President Grover Cleveland. Sara came from a wealthy shipping family. She raised Franklin and helped him with his studies.

As a young boy, private teachers educated Franklin at home. The family often traveled to Europe. They also took vacations to Campobello Island in Canada. There, Franklin began his lifelong love of sailing. Franklin also enjoyed stamp collecting and bird-watching throughout his life.

FAST FACTS

BORN - January 30, 1882

WIFE - Anna Eleanor Roosevelt (1884–1962)

CHILDREN - 6

POLITICAL PARTY - Democrat

AGE AT INAUGURATION - 51

YEARS SERVED - 1933–1945

VICE PRESIDENTS - John Nance Garner, Henry A. Wallace, Harry S. Truman

DIED - April 12, 1945, age 63

When he was 14, Franklin entered Groton School in Groton, Massachusetts. This was a boarding school for young men. There, Franklin earned average grades. He also was the student manager of the baseball team.

Franklin's parents expected good behavior from their son. He respected their rules. So, he rarely got into trouble at home or at school.

COLLEGE AND MARRIAGE

After graduation, Roosevelt went to Harvard University in Cambridge, Massachusetts. He studied history, **economics**, and science. Roosevelt also became president and editor of the school newspaper, the *Crimson*.

Then in 1904, Roosevelt began law school. He attended Columbia University Law School in New York City, New York.

On March 17, 1905, he married Anna Eleanor Roosevelt. She went by Eleanor. President Theodore Roosevelt was her uncle. He gave Eleanor away at the couple's wedding.

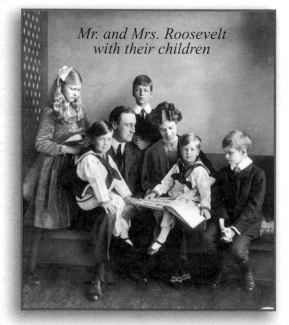

Mr. and Mrs. Roosevelt with their children

The Roosevelts had six children. Anna Eleanor was born in 1906. James was born in 1907, followed by Elliot in 1910. Franklin Jr. was born in 1914, and John was born in 1916. The Roosevelts had another son, but he died in 1909 while still a baby.

10

Mr. and Mrs. Roosevelt often visited Springwood, the Roosevelt family estate in Hyde Park.

STATE SENATOR

Roosevelt never graduated from Columbia. Instead, he passed the test to become a lawyer in 1907. Roosevelt then began working for Carter, Ledyard, and Milburn. Yet, he found his work at this New York City law firm boring. Roosevelt began thinking about working in politics.

Democratic Party leaders believed Roosevelt could be successful in New York politics. He had a well-known name. And, he had the wealth to run a strong campaign.

Roosevelt jumped at the chance to serve the public. He had learned from Theodore Roosevelt that political work was exciting and meaningful. So in 1910, he ran for state senator.

Roosevelt was an energetic candidate. He toured the district by car and made many speeches. The voters liked what they heard. They elected him by more than 1,000 votes.

As a state senator, Roosevelt worked hard. He favored giving women the right to vote. Roosevelt also supported workers and

As a state senator, Roosevelt represented the area around Hyde Park.

farmers. He voted to limit the workweek to 54 hours for boys aged 16 to 21. And, he supported protecting soil. In 1912, Roosevelt was reelected.

LEADING THE NAVY

Also in 1912, Roosevelt worked for Woodrow Wilson's presidential campaign. Roosevelt made speeches and wrote letters. He also led 150 Wilson supporters at the **Democratic National Convention**. Wilson won the election.

Roosevelt's work impressed President Wilson and **Democratic** Party leaders. So in 1913, Wilson named Roosevelt assistant secretary of the navy.

Roosevelt worked well with admirals, navy department employees, and party leaders. He kept the navy prepared. And, he looked for ways to improve it.

In 1914, Roosevelt wanted to run for the U.S. Senate. However, he did not win the Democratic nomination. So, Roosevelt remained assistant secretary of the navy. That year, **World War I** began in Europe.

The United States entered World War I in 1917. Roosevelt openly supported the war. He worked hard to make the navy bigger and stronger. And in 1918, he visited the troops in Europe.

By the end of the war, Roosevelt had gained valuable experience. He had made important political connections and had become known nationally. Roosevelt was ready to run for a higher political office.

Roosevelt (left) *followed in Theodore Roosevelt's footsteps. Both men served as assistant secretary of the navy before becoming president.*

UNEXPECTED CHALLENGES

In 1920, the **Democratic** Party chose Ohio governor James M. Cox to run for president. Roosevelt became his **running mate**. He and Cox ran against **Republican** Warren G. Harding. Harding's running mate was Calvin Coolidge.

Roosevelt ran another strong, energetic campaign. He traveled the country making more than 1,000 speeches. Cox and Roosevelt lost the election. Still, people believed Roosevelt had a successful political career ahead of him.

Then in August 1921, Roosevelt became ill at Campobello Island. He became partially **paralyzed** and learned he had **polio**. Never again would he walk without help.

Roosevelt's political career seemed to be over. Yet with Mrs. Roosevelt's help, he fought to recover. In 1924, Roosevelt went to Warm Springs, Georgia. There, he treated his paralysis in warm mineral water.

Soon, Roosevelt decided to help other **polio** sufferers. In 1927, he formed the Georgia Warm Springs Foundation. Roosevelt hired doctors to provide affordable treatment. Like Roosevelt, the patients swam in the warm mineral water.

Meanwhile, Roosevelt kept active in politics. He wrote many letters to party leaders. He often met with them in Washington, D.C., on his way to and from Warm Springs.

Roosevelt's cottage at Warm Springs, Georgia, became known as the "Little White House."

GOVERNOR ROOSEVELT

In 1928, the **Democrats** asked Roosevelt to run for governor of New York. Roosevelt easily won the election. He defeated state **attorney general** Albert Ottinger by 25,000 votes.

Governor Roosevelt passed more laws that reduced working hours. He also supported lowering the cost of electricity. And, he passed laws to help poor farmers move to better land. In 1930, Roosevelt was reelected by 725,000 votes. It was the biggest election victory in state history.

By 1931, Americans were suffering through the **Great Depression**. Many New Yorkers were out of work. So, Governor Roosevelt formed a program to help those who needed jobs. It was called the Temporary Emergency Relief Administration.

In 1932, the Democratic Party nominated Roosevelt to run for president. His **running mate** was Texas representative John Nance Garner. Roosevelt flew to the **Democratic National Convention** in Chicago, Illinois, to address the party.

Roosevelt's 1932 presidential campaign took him to 38 states.

This was unusual. However, Roosevelt wanted to show he had recovered his strength after his illness. There he said, "I pledge you, I pledge myself, to a new deal for the American people."

Roosevelt traveled the country giving speeches. Americans believed his New Deal was the answer to helping the **economy** recover. In November 1932, Roosevelt and Garner defeated President Herbert Hoover. They won 472 electoral votes to Hoover's 59.

PRESIDENT ROOSEVELT

On March 4, 1933, Roosevelt was **inaugurated** at the U.S. Capitol in Washington, D.C. There he said, "The only thing we have to fear is fear itself." Roosevelt's speech gave Americans hope.

The first three months of Roosevelt's first term became known as the Hundred Days. During this time, many of his New Deal programs were created. This included the Agricultural Adjustment Administration. It limited the amount of crops farmers could grow. This kept crop prices from falling, which helped farmers make money.

The Civilian Conservation Corps (CCC) also formed during the Hundred Days. This organization helped preserve the nation's natural resources. The CCC gave jobs to young men. They planted trees, built dams, and created campgrounds.

SUPREME COURT APPOINTMENTS

HUGO L. BLACK - 1937

STANLEY F. REED - 1938

FELIX FRANKFURTER - 1939

WILLIAM O. DOUGLAS - 1939

FRANK MURPHY - 1940

HARLAN FISKE STONE - 1941

JAMES F. BYRNES - 1941

ROBERT H. JACKSON - 1941

WILEY B. RUTLEDGE - 1943

Men also found jobs with the new Tennessee Valley Authority. This New Deal program focused on flood control. Eventually, it also provided affordable electricity to seven states.

In 1935, Roosevelt continued to create programs with the Second New Deal. The Works Progress Administration created jobs for millions of people. Some workers built bridges, roads, and airports. Others collected local histories or created art for their communities.

President Roosevelt also signed the Social Security Act into law. This provided money for people who could not find jobs or were retired. It also helped people pay for medical care. The Wagner Act also passed in 1935. It established certain rights for laborers.

As time passed, the federal government was becoming more powerful. Some people felt Roosevelt was abusing his power. They claimed Roosevelt's programs were **unconstitutional**. So, several New Deal programs ended. Yet many remained in place even after he left office.

Vice President John Nance Garner

In 1936, President Roosevelt and Vice President Garner were up for reelection. They defeated Kansas governor Alfred M. Landon. Roosevelt received 523 electoral votes, while Landon received just 8. This was one of the biggest election victories in U.S. history.

PRESIDENT ROOSEVELT'S CABINET

FIRST TERM
MARCH 4, 1933–JANUARY 20, 1937

- **STATE** – Cordell Hull
- **TREASURY** – W.H. Woodin
  Henry Morgenthau Jr. (from January 8, 1934)
- **WAR** – George H. Dern
- **NAVY** – Claude A. Swanson
- **ATTORNEY GENERAL** – Homer S. Cummings
- **INTERIOR** – Harold L. Ickes
- **AGRICULTURE** – Henry A. Wallace
- **COMMERCE** – Daniel C. Roper
- **LABOR** – Frances Perkins

THIRD TERM
JANUARY 20, 1941–JANUARY 20, 1945

- **STATE** – Cordell Hull
  Edward R. Stettinius (from December 1, 1944)
- **TREASURY** – Henry Morgenthau Jr.
- **WAR** – Henry L. Stimson
- **NAVY** – Frank Knox
  James Forrestal (from May 18, 1944)
- **ATTORNEY GENERAL** – Robert H. Jackson
  Francis Biddle (from September 5, 1941)
- **INTERIOR** – Harold L. Ickes
- **AGRICULTURE** – Claude R. Wickard
- **COMMERCE** – Jesse H. Jones
- **LABOR** – Frances Perkins

SECOND TERM
JANUARY 20, 1937–JANUARY 20, 1941

- **STATE** – Cordell Hull
- **TREASURY** – Henry Morgenthau Jr.
- **WAR** – Harry H. Woodring, Henry L. Stimson (from July 10, 1940)
- **NAVY** – Claude A. Swanson, Charles Edison (from January 11, 1940)
  Frank Knox (from July 10, 1940)
- **ATTORNEY GENERAL** – Homer S. Cummings
  Frank Murphy (from January 17, 1939)
  Robert H. Jackson (from January 18, 1940)
- **INTERIOR** – Harold L. Ickes
- **AGRICULTURE** – Henry A. Wallace
  Claude R. Wickard (from September 5, 1940)
- **COMMERCE** – Daniel C. Roper
  Harry L. Hopkins (from January 23, 1939)
  Jesse H. Jones (from September 19, 1940)
- **LABOR** – Frances Perkins

FOURTH TERM
JANUARY 20, 1945–APRIL 12, 1945

- **STATE** – Edward R. Stettinius
- **TREASURY** – Henry Morgenthau Jr.
- **WAR** – Henry L. Stimson
- **NAVY** – James Forrestal
- **ATTORNEY GENERAL** – Francis Biddle
- **INTERIOR** – Harold L. Ickes
- **AGRICULTURE** – Claude R. Wickard
- **COMMERCE** – Jesse H. Jones
  Henry A. Wallace (from March 2, 1945)
- **LABOR** – Frances Perkins

WORLD WAR II

In 1940, President Roosevelt thought about retiring. However, he felt a sense of duty to continue as president. But no U.S. president had ever served more than two terms.

That year, the **Democrats** broke tradition and nominated Roosevelt for a third term. His new **running mate** was Henry A. Wallace. More than 49 million people voted in the election. President Roosevelt defeated Wendell Willkie to win his third term.

World War II had begun in 1939. Germany had seized much of Europe. Now, Germany was threatening Great Britain. The British fought hard, but they needed supplies. Roosevelt felt that if Britain was seized, the United States would be at risk.

Vice President Henry A. Wallace

24

Many Americans did not want to join the war. So after the election, Roosevelt arranged the Lend-Lease Act. It became law on March 11, 1941.

According to the act, the United States would lend supplies to the **Allies** fighting Germany. This included ships, airplanes, weapons, food, and clothing. The United States would also repair ships and train soldiers. Now, the United States could help Great Britain without officially joining the war.

Roosevelt signing the Lend-Lease Act

The United States could not stay out of **World War II** for long. On December 7, 1941, Japanese airplanes staged a surprise attack on the U.S. naval base at Pearl Harbor, Hawaii. They sank ships, destroyed airplanes, and killed more than 2,000 Americans.

Harry S. Truman served as the thirty-third U.S. president from 1945 to 1953.

The next day, President Roosevelt asked Congress to declare war on Japan. By December 11, the United States was also at war with Germany and Italy.

Roosevelt traveled the world to meet with other leaders. He helped keep the **Allies** united in their war against the **Axis Powers**.

Another presidential election took place in 1944. Roosevelt was in poor health. Still, he believed he should remain president. The

United States was still fighting the war. Yet the **Axis Powers** had suffered major defeats.

Roosevelt's new **running mate** was Harry S. Truman. Their opponent was New York governor Thomas E. Dewey. For the first time in U.S. history, a president was elected to a fourth term. Roosevelt earned 432 electoral votes to Dewey's 99.

DRAFT No. 1

December 7, 1941.

PROPOSED MESSAGE TO THE CONGRESS

Yesterday, December 7, 1941, a date which will live in infamy the United States of America was suddenly and deliberately attacked by naval and air forces of the Empire of Japan.

The United States was at the moment at peace with that nation and was still in conversation with its Government and its Emperor looking toward the maintenance of peace in the Pacific. Indeed, one hour after Japanese air squadrons had commenced bombing in Oahu the Japanese Ambassador to the United States and his colleague delivered to the Secretary of State a formal reply to a recent American message. While this reply stated that it seemed useless to continue the existing diplomatic negotiations, it contained no threat or hint of war or armed attack.

It will be recorded that the distance of Hawaii from Japan makes it obvious that the attack was deliberately planned many days or even weeks ago. During the intervening time the Japanese Government has deliberately sought to deceive the United States by false statements and expressions of hope for continued peace.

In his famous speech to Congress, Roosevelt called December 7 "a date which will live in infamy."

FINAL DAYS

When Roosevelt's fourth term began, **World War II** was almost over. In February 1945, Roosevelt attended the Yalta Conference in the Crimea. This is in present-day southern Ukraine.

There, he met with Prime Minister Winston Churchill of Great Britain. Premier Joseph Stalin of the Soviet Union joined them. Together, these **Allied** leaders discussed plans for the end of the war. They also discussed Europe's future and what would soon become the **United Nations**.

After the conference, Roosevelt returned to the United States. In April, he traveled to Warm Springs. On April 12, Roosevelt was reading papers while a painter sketched him. Suddenly, he complained of a pain in his head. He then collapsed. A few hours later, President Franklin D. Roosevelt died. That evening, Truman was sworn in as president.

Roosevelt's death shocked the nation. He had been the country's leader for 12 years. Crowds lined the train route as

Roosevelt was brought back to New York. He was buried at his home in Hyde Park on April 15, 1945.

Franklin D. Roosevelt was one of America's most important presidents. He led the country for longer than any president before or since. He fought to end the **Great Depression** and **World War II**. Not everyone agreed with his policies. Yet Roosevelt was seen as a great and beloved leader.

Left to right: *Churchill, Roosevelt, and Stalin at the Yalta Conference. During World War II, these world leaders were called the "Big Three."*

OFFICE OF THE PRESIDENT

BRANCHES OF GOVERNMENT

The U.S. government is divided into three branches. They are the executive, legislative, and judicial branches. This division is called a separation of powers. Each branch has some power over the others. This is called a system of checks and balances.

EXECUTIVE BRANCH

The executive branch enforces laws. It is made up of the president, the vice president, and the president's cabinet. The president represents the United States around the world. He or she oversees relations with other countries and signs treaties. The president signs bills into law and appoints officials and federal judges. He or she also leads the military and manages government workers.

LEGISLATIVE BRANCH

The legislative branch makes laws, maintains the military, and regulates trade. It also has the power to declare war. This branch consists of the Senate and the House of Representatives. Together, these two houses make up Congress. Each state has two senators. A state's population determines the number of representatives it has.

JUDICIAL BRANCH

The judicial branch interprets laws. It consists of district courts, courts of appeals, and the Supreme Court. District courts try cases. If a person disagrees with a trial's outcome, he or she may appeal. If the courts of appeals support the ruling, a person may appeal to the Supreme Court. The Supreme Court also makes sure that laws follow the U.S. Constitution.

Qualifications for Office

To be president, a person must meet three requirements. A candidate must be at least 35 years old and a natural-born U.S. citizen. He or she must also have lived in the United States for at least 14 years.

Electoral College

The U.S. presidential election is an indirect election. Voters from each state choose electors to represent them in the Electoral College. The number of electors from each state is based on population. Each elector has one electoral vote. Electors are pledged to cast their vote for the candidate who receives the highest number of popular votes in their state. A candidate must receive the majority of Electoral College votes to win.

Term of Office

Each president may be elected to two four-year terms. Sometimes, a president may only be elected once. This happens if he or she served more than two years of the previous president's term.

The presidential election is held on the Tuesday after the first Monday in November. The president is sworn in on January 20 of the following year. At that time, he or she takes the oath of office:

I do solemnly swear (or affirm) that I will faithfully execute the office of President of the United States, and will to the best of my ability, preserve, protect and defend the Constitution of the United States.

LINE OF SUCCESSION

The Presidential Succession Act of 1947 defines who becomes president if the president cannot serve. The vice president is first in the line of succession. Next are the Speaker of the House and the President Pro Tempore of the Senate. If none of these individuals is able to serve, the office falls to the president's cabinet members. They would take office in the order in which each department was created:

Secretary of State

Secretary of the Treasury

Secretary of Defense

Attorney General

Secretary of the Interior

Secretary of Agriculture

Secretary of Commerce

Secretary of Labor

Secretary of Health and Human Services

Secretary of Housing and Urban Development

Secretary of Transportation

Secretary of Energy

Secretary of Education

Secretary of Veterans Affairs

Secretary of Homeland Security

BENEFITS

- While in office, the president receives a salary of $400,000 each year. He or she lives in the White House and has 24-hour Secret Service protection.

- The president may travel on a Boeing 747 jet called Air Force One. The airplane can accommodate 70 passengers. It has kitchens, a dining room, sleeping areas, and a conference room. It also has fully equipped offices with the latest communications systems. Air Force One can fly halfway around the world before needing to refuel. It can even refuel in flight!

- If the president wishes to travel by car, he or she uses Cadillac One. Cadillac One is a Cadillac Deville. It has been modified with heavy armor and communications systems. The president takes Cadillac One along when visiting other countries if secure transportation will be needed.

- The president also travels on a helicopter called Marine One. Like the presidential car, Marine One accompanies the president when traveling abroad if necessary.

- Sometimes, the president needs to get away and relax with family and friends. Camp David is the official presidential retreat. It is located in the cool, wooded mountains in Maryland. The U.S. Navy maintains the retreat, and the U.S. Marine Corps keeps it secure. The camp offers swimming, tennis, golf, and hiking.

- When the president leaves office, he or she receives Secret Service protection for ten more years. He or she also receives a yearly pension of $191,300 and funding for office space, supplies, and staff.

PRESIDENTS AND THEIR TERMS

PRESIDENT	PARTY	TOOK OFFICE	LEFT OFFICE	TERMS SERVED	VICE PRESIDENT
George Washington	None	April 30, 1789	March 4, 1797	Two	John Adams
John Adams	Federalist	March 4, 1797	March 4, 1801	One	Thomas Jefferson
Thomas Jefferson	Democratic-Republican	March 4, 1801	March 4, 1809	Two	Aaron Burr, George Clinton
James Madison	Democratic-Republican	March 4, 1809	March 4, 1817	Two	George Clinton, Elbridge Gerry
James Monroe	Democratic-Republican	March 4, 1817	March 4, 1825	Two	Daniel D. Tompkins
John Quincy Adams	Democratic-Republican	March 4, 1825	March 4, 1829	One	John C. Calhoun
Andrew Jackson	Democrat	March 4, 1829	March 4, 1837	Two	John C. Calhoun, Martin Van Buren
Martin Van Buren	Democrat	March 4, 1837	March 4, 1841	One	Richard M. Johnson
William H. Harrison	Whig	March 4, 1841	April 4, 1841	Died During First Term	John Tyler
John Tyler	Whig	April 6, 1841	March 4, 1845	Completed Harrison's Term	Office Vacant
James K. Polk	Democrat	March 4, 1845	March 4, 1849	One	George M. Dallas
Zachary Taylor	Whig	March 5, 1849	July 9, 1850	Died During First Term	Millard Fillmore

PRESIDENT	PARTY	TOOK OFFICE	LEFT OFFICE	TERMS SERVED	VICE PRESIDENT
Millard Fillmore	Whig	July 10, 1850	March 4, 1853	Completed Taylor's Term	Office Vacant
Franklin Pierce	Democrat	March 4, 1853	March 4, 1857	One	William R.D. King
James Buchanan	Democrat	March 4, 1857	March 4, 1861	One	John C. Breckinridge
Abraham Lincoln	Republican	March 4, 1861	April 15, 1865	Served One Term, Died During Second Term	Hannibal Hamlin, Andrew Johnson
Andrew Johnson	Democrat	April 15, 1865	March 4, 1869	Completed Lincoln's Second Term	Office Vacant
Ulysses S. Grant	Republican	March 4, 1869	March 4, 1877	Two	Schuyler Colfax, Henry Wilson
Rutherford B. Hayes	Republican	March 3, 1877	March 4, 1881	One	William A. Wheeler
James A. Garfield	Republican	March 4, 1881	September 19, 1881	Died During First Term	Chester Arthur
Chester Arthur	Republican	September 20, 1881	March 4, 1885	Completed Garfield's Term	Office Vacant
Grover Cleveland	Democrat	March 4, 1885	March 4, 1889	One	Thomas A. Hendricks
Benjamin Harrison	Republican	March 4, 1889	March 4, 1893	One	Levi P. Morton
Grover Cleveland	Democrat	March 4, 1893	March 4, 1897	One	Adlai E. Stevenson
William McKinley	Republican	March 4, 1897	September 14, 1901	Served One Term, Died During Second Term	Garret A. Hobart, Theodore Roosevelt

PRESIDENT	PARTY	TOOK OFFICE	LEFT OFFICE	TERMS SERVED	VICE PRESIDENT
Theodore Roosevelt	Republican	September 14, 1901	March 4, 1909	Completed McKinley's Second Term, Served One Term	Office Vacant, Charles Fairbanks
William Taft	Republican	March 4, 1909	March 4, 1913	One	James S. Sherman
Woodrow Wilson	Democrat	March 4, 1913	March 4, 1921	Two	Thomas R. Marshall
Warren G. Harding	Republican	March 4, 1921	August 2, 1923	Died During First Term	Calvin Coolidge
Calvin Coolidge	Republican	August 3, 1923	March 4, 1929	Completed Harding's Term, Served One Term	Office Vacant, Charles Dawes
Herbert Hoover	Republican	March 4, 1929	March 4, 1933	One	Charles Curtis
Franklin D. Roosevelt	Democrat	March 4, 1933	April 12, 1945	Served Three Terms, Died During Fourth Term	John Nance Garner, Henry A. Wallace, Harry S. Truman
Harry S. Truman	Democrat	April 12, 1945	January 20, 1953	Completed Roosevelt's Fourth Term, Served One Term	Office Vacant, Alben Barkley
Dwight D. Eisenhower	Republican	January 20, 1953	January 20, 1961	Two	Richard Nixon
John F. Kennedy	Democrat	January 20, 1961	November 22, 1963	Died During First Term	Lyndon B. Johnson
Lyndon B. Johnson	Democrat	November 22, 1963	January 20, 1969	Completed Kennedy's Term, Served One Term	Office Vacant, Hubert H. Humphrey
Richard Nixon	Republican	January 20, 1969	August 9, 1974	Completed First Term, Resigned During Second Term	Spiro T. Agnew, Gerald Ford

PRESIDENT	PARTY	TOOK OFFICE	LEFT OFFICE	TERMS SERVED	VICE PRESIDENT
Gerald Ford	Republican	August 9, 1974	January 20, 1977	Completed Nixon's Second Term	Nelson A. Rockefeller
Jimmy Carter	Democrat	January 20, 1977	January 20, 1981	One	Walter Mondale
Ronald Reagan	Republican	January 20, 1981	January 20, 1989	Two	George H.W. Bush
George H.W. Bush	Republican	January 20, 1989	January 20, 1993	One	Dan Quayle
Bill Clinton	Democrat	January 20, 1993	January 20, 2001	Two	Al Gore
George W. Bush	Republican	January 20, 2001	January 20, 2009	Two	Dick Cheney
Barack Obama	Democrat	January 20, 2009			Joe Biden

"The love of freedom is still fierce and steady in the nation today." Franklin D. Roosevelt

WRITE TO THE PRESIDENT

You may write to the president at:

**The White House
1600 Pennsylvania Avenue NW
Washington, DC 20500**

You may e-mail the president at:
comments@whitehouse.gov

GLOSSARY

allies - people, groups, or nations united for some special purpose. During World War II Great Britain, France, the United States, and the Soviet Union were called the Allies.

attorney general - the chief law officer of a national or state government.

Axis Powers - countries that fought together during World War II. Germany, Italy, and Japan were called the Axis Powers.

Democrat - a member of the Democratic political party. Democrats believe in social change and strong government.

Democratic National Convention - a national meeting held every four years during which the Democratic Party chooses its candidates for president and vice president.

economy - the way a nation uses its money, goods, and natural resources. Economics is the science of this.

Great Depression - the period from 1929 to 1942 of worldwide economic trouble when there was little buying or selling, and many people could not find work.

inaugurate (ih-NAW-gyuh-rayt) - to swear into a political office.

paralyze - to cause a loss of motion or feeling in a part of the body.

polio - the common name for poliomyelitis, a disease that sometimes leaves people paralyzed. It usually affects children.

Republican - a member of the Republican political party. Republicans are conservative and believe in small government.

running mate - a candidate running for a lower-rank position on an election ticket, especially the candidate for vice president.

unconstitutional - something that goes against the laws of a constitution.

United Nations - a group of nations formed in 1945. Its goals are peace, human rights, security, and social and economic development.

World War I - from 1914 to 1918, fought in Europe. Great Britain, France, Russia, the United States, and their allies were on one side. Germany, Austria-Hungary, and their allies were on the other side.

World War II - from 1939 to 1945, fought in Europe, Asia, and Africa. Great Britain, France, the United States, the Soviet Union, and their allies were on one side. Germany, Italy, Japan, and their allies were on the other side.

WEB SITES

To learn more about Franklin D. Roosevelt, visit ABDO Publishing Company on the World Wide Web at **www.abdopublishing.com**. Web sites about Franklin D. Roosevelt are featured on our Book Links page. These links are routinely monitored and updated to provide the most current information available.

INDEX